The Wild Caves

Written by Jenny Feely

Illustrated by Naomi Lewis

Flying Start
to Literacy®

Contents

Chapter 1

A doorway to a new world

Hassan and Ferah were fetching buckets of water when suddenly they heard a terrific rumble. A huge cloud of dust was coming out of the cave where they lived.

"Oh, no!" yelled Ferah. "Cave-in!"

"Dad's in there!" yelled her brother, Hassan, as he started to run toward the cave.

This was one of the dangers of living underground – sometimes there were cave-ins. Hassan and Ferah's dad had been digging out a new storage room for their family. Excavating was always a dangerous job.

Hassan and Ferah were trying to decide what to do when out of the clouds of dust walked their dad, coughing and shaking dust out of his hair.

"I'm okay," he said. "But the storage room will have to go somewhere else."

Hassan and Ferah loved living underground. There were hundreds of different rooms in the caves, connected by lots and lots of doorways, tunnels and stairways. It was cool when the hot summer sun baked the ground outside and warm in the freezing winters.

The caves had everything the people needed to survive. There were stables for the animals and huge storage rooms that were just the right temperature to keep food in good condition. And there were pits to store water – it was Hassan and Ferah's job to keep their family's pit filled with water from the river below.

Sometimes the winter snow piled up outside the cave mouth and no one could get out for weeks at a time. This meant that the family had to survive on the food they had stored. That's why Dad was excavating a new, bigger storage room – so that they could store more food.

When the dust cleared, Hassan, Ferah and Dad went back into the cave.

"Look what I found," said Dad.

Hassan and Ferah couldn't believe their eyes. The storage room Dad had begun digging opened into a long tunnel.

"Where does it go?" asked Ferah.

"I'm not sure," said Dad. "I will go and explore when I get time. But you two must stay out. This tunnel is probably one of many natural tunnels linking up inside the mountain – I think it's part of a wild cave system."

"Wild caves?" asked Hassan, his eyes lighting up. "What are they?"

"Wild caves weren't made by people digging," said Dad. "They were made by nature. But wild caves are dangerous places. People get lost in them and are never seen again."

Just then, Hassan and Ferah's little brother Garni came running into the cave.

"Look!" he cried, holding up an ordinary yellowish rock. "I found another special rock for my collection." Garni dropped the rock into his bag.

"Well, that's a start, Garni," said Dad. "Now you three can help me clear the rest of these rocks out of the cave."

Hassan and Ferah groaned and began filling buckets with the rocks. They wished they could explore the new tunnel instead.

Chapter 2
Into the darkness

Every night after they had finished their day's chores, Ferah and Hassan talked about the mysterious tunnel and where it might lead. They longed to go exploring, but they knew it was too dangerous and they could not disobey their father.

Soon the day came for the midsummer festival. It was a grand celebration that was held down on the banks of the river each year. Everyone looked forward to the huge bonfire, the dancing and the enormous feast later in the evening.

The midsummer festival was the perfect entertainment for Hassan and Ferah – but Dad had told them they must take Garni with them and look after him for the day. Hassan and Ferah couldn't believe it – Garni was such a baby, they didn't want to be stuck with him. But they had no choice.

The three children were headed down to the banks of the river where the festival was being held, when suddenly Garni cried out.

"Oh, no, I forgot my special rock collection," he said, turning around and bolting back toward the caves.

"Garni, come back here!" called Hassan.

But it was too late. Garni had already started running back to the cave. Ferah and Hassan followed him, but when they got into the cave, Garni was nowhere to be seen.

"Garni!" they called, looking down each passage in the cave. But he was gone. Then they noticed Garni's hat on the ground in the entrance to the new tunnel.

"He's gone in here!" said Hassan, alarmed.

"We have to find him now!" said Ferah. "If he goes too deep, he'll be lost in the wild caves forever."

Hassan and Ferah lit a candle and hurried through the entrance.

Soon they came to a fork in the tunnel.

"Which way do we go?" said Hassan.

"Left and up," said Ferah.

"Why?" asked Hassan.

"Garni likes to climb," said Ferah. "Do you have a better idea?"

"No," said Hassan.

But it wasn't long before they reached another fork. This time, four tunnels went off in different directions. Hassan and Ferah looked at each other. Then they both started calling out to their little brother.

"Garni!" they yelled. "Garni, where are you?"

But there was no answer, only silence.

Ferah sat down on a ledge at the mouth of one of the tunnels, holding the candle. "What should we do?" she sighed. "If we go the wrong way, we'll never find him, and we may never find our way back either."

But Hassan wasn't listening. He was staring at something next to Ferah's hand. Ferah looked down. The candlelight flickered across a small, yellowish rock.

"Garni's rock!" she said. "He's gone this way!"

The children walked on and on, taking tunnels to the left and to the right, all the time following the trail of rocks that Garni had left. Finally, they saw a flicker of candlelight up ahead.

"Garni," Ferah called. "Is that you?"

The candlelight stopped moving.

"Ferah?" a timid voice said from the darkness.

"It is him!" shouted Hassan, and they both ran toward the candle, finding their little brother and embracing him.

"I went looking for rocks for my collection," said Garni, "but I think I went too far."

Chapter 3
Lost in the dark

Just then the candles started to flicker. Hassan quickly put his hand around his candle, but he was too late. The candles went out, leaving the three children in the dark.

"Now what will we do?" asked Hassan.

"I don't know," said Ferah.

Garni began to cry. "I left my rocks in a trail that we could follow back," he sobbed. "But without the light from the candles we will never find them!"

"We're lost," said Hassan sitting on a rock.

"Someone will come and find us," said Ferah.

"How can they?" said Hassan, sounding worried. "No one knows where we are."

"Think," said Ferah. "There must be something we can do."

"But what?" said Hassan.

"Oh, I wish the candles hadn't blown out," said Garni.

"That's it," said Ferah. "Why did the candles go out? The air in this tunnel is moving. There must be an opening near here. All we have to do is walk toward the breeze."

The children stumbled along, always facing into the breeze. The breeze got stronger and stronger. And then faintly, in the distance, there was a light.

"We're saved!" yelled Hassan, running toward the light.

They stepped out of the cave and saw that they were high up on the side of the mountain. Far below them on the banks of the river they could see the midsummer festival.

They started their slow, careful descent down the mountain, placing their feet carefully on the rocks and holding onto tufts of grass. It took a long time, but finally they reached the festival at the bottom. Dad saw them and waved.

"Having a good time at the festival?" he called, surprised when the three children rushed over and hugged him.

Chapter 4
Trapped!

That night in the children's family cave there was a big feast. Hassan and Ferah's aunts and uncles and cousins and neighbours were all there.

Suddenly, there was a loud, terrifying rumble. They knew just what it was. They all looked up to see a huge cloud of dust. The rocks above the mouth of the cave had caved in and blocked the entrance.

"We can dig our way out," said the men. But as soon as they started to move the bigger rocks to clear the entrance, smaller ones fell in their place.

"We'll all die in here," said one woman.

"No, we won't," said Ferah. "Follow us, we know another way, if it is still open."

"Yes," said Hassan. "We can go through the wild caves. It is a long way, but it can be done."

"How do you know?" asked their dad. "It's dangerous in there."

"Garni went into the tunnel and we had to save him," said Ferah. "That's how we know."

"Then you must lead us," said their dad. Everyone followed Hassan and Ferah into the tunnel.

"Which way?" their father asked at the first turn.

"Left and up," said Ferah.

Soon they reached the place with the four pathways. All the people looked at each other.

Then Garni pushed through to the front of the crowd excitedly.

"I know the way!" said Garni. "It is the left tunnel. I put one of my special stones at every turn we took. Follow the stones and we will find the way out."

And so the people followed the trail of Garni's stones to safety.

A note from the author

After reading the book *Incredible Underground Homes,* I did some research to find out what it would be like to live under the ground.

As I learned about amazing underground cities and homes built into cliffs, I began to think about what it would be like for children who lived in such homes. To add some drama to the story, I wondered about what people who live in caves would fear the most.

I decided that if I lived in a cave, I would be most worried about cave-ins. What would happen if there was a cave-in? How would the people survive? These questions gave me the idea for this story.